# RING ᴛʜᴇ BELL

## Literacy Is Everyone's Problem

**Ring The Bell: Literacy Is Everyone's Problem**

Copyright © 2019 by Karessa Morrow

All rights reserved. No part of this publication may be reproduced, stored, in a retrieval system, or transmitted in any form or by any means-for example, electronic, photocopy, and recording-without the prior written permission of the author. The only exception is brief quotations in printed reviews.

The Library of Congress has catalogued this book under the following:

Morrow, Karessa

Ring The Bell/Karessa Morrow

Library of Congress Control Number: 2019933113

ISBN 978-1-7335684-0-1 (Paperback)

Printed in the United States of America

"The mediocre teacher tells. The good teacher explains. The superior teacher demonstrates. The great teacher inspires."
   --William A. Ward

## Dedication

This book is dedicated to all educators. Our students need to know that you believe education is important and that you want them to do well in school. High expectations set the stage for academic success! I am confident that this book will help your students to maximize their reading skills.

# Acknowledgements

This BOOK IS A CELEBRATION of faith, family, friends, and colleagues who helped shape my thoughts into an excellent book of which I am most proud.

I would like to thank my mother, Mattie Jewell Morrow for a lifetime of selflessness, love, and support. I learned the meaning of hard work by watching you! I would like to thank my sister Deborah Phillips and my brother-in-law Clayton Phillips, for their words of wisdom and encouragement throughout the years and for always being there for me whenever I needed them. I would like to extend special thanks to my mentor, who has aided me in the development of this book, Dr. Catherine Bear, Associate Professor at Maryville University in St. Louis, Missouri. Last but certainly not least, I would like to thank Linda Bell, Regional Institute of Tutorial Education Project Coordinator at the University of Missouri-St. Louis for her unrelenting support and for providing meaningful feedback.

# Foreword

It is with great humility, that I write this foreword for my sister's first publication. I always knew that she would accomplish whatever dream she has set before her. This is another task conquered.

I consider it a pure joy and blessing for her to share with each reader the three decades of her work in the area of education. This book has given me more insight on how to improve my grandson's reading ability and to ensure that he reads on grade level. Enjoy!


Deborah Phillips, M.S.N.C.C.

## Table of Contents

Chapter 1: The Literacy Crisis……………………………………..1

Chapter 2: Changing the Trajectory of the School to Prison Pipeline……………………………………………………………..8

Chapter 3: The Journey to Reading Proficiency………………..24

Chapter 4: Third Grade Matters: The Reading Milestone……..46

Chapter 5: Building Our Literacy Model………………………….55

Chapter 6: High Achievement Starts at Home………………….63

Chapter 7: Epilogue and Reflections…………………………….76

Appendix A: 20 ways to Encourage Reading ………………….89

Appendix B: Reading Tips for Parents………………………….93

Appendix C: Parental Involvement is Key to Student Success….95

Appendix D: Tips for an Involved Parent……………………….98

Bibliography……………………………………………………….100

*"There's no such thing as a kid who hates reading. There are kids who love reading, and kids who are reading the wrong books." --James Patterson*

# Chapter 1
## *The Literacy Crisis*

Today, educators need to focus on literacy instruction in elementary, middle school and high school because never before in history has literacy—the ability to read, think, write, and speak in the academic disciplines—been such a basic necessity on such a massive scale. The demands of the 21st century university and workforce are raising the literacy stakes for young people across the country. In response to these rigorous demands, most U.S. states have focused their school systems on college- and career-readiness. Many have adopted the Common Core State Standards, which "ask students to demonstrate deep conceptual understanding through the application of content knowledge," (Day-Bullmaster, 2014). Some states that have chosen not to adopt the Common Core State Standards have implemented their own set of rigorous standards designed to prepare students for college and the workplace. After high school graduation, K-12 students, regardless of where they come from and where their career paths lead, will be expected to read more complex texts, do more with different types of texts, and handle larger amounts of reading. Ensuring that all students acquire the literacy skills they need to compete and thrive in the world they will face is a moral imperative for educators, policy makers and families. Failing to live up to this imperative is simply not an option!

I will always remember sitting in a principal leadership professional development training with my peers discussing one important question, "Are schools responsible for the prison pipeline?" In my mind, the answer is a resounding, "Yes!" I do believe that *failing* schools are responsible for the school to prison pipeline, and that this phenomenon is something we can most certainly control.

The professional development training that day made me reflect on my leadership style and my role as a principal, and it became deeply personal. I believe a principal's role is about making a difference in the lives of children. Leading and teaching is challenging work that requires a high level of understanding and patience. I had to do everything within my power to make sure that *our* school did not fail *our* children! This motivated me to begin my journey to ensure all kids in my school would be reading on grade level. My favorite quote was, "Failure is not an option!"

I knew that focusing on building the capacity of my teachers was the first order of business. I had read numerous studies concluding that a teacher's expectations has a huge impact on student achievement. The best teachers have high expectations for all of their students. They expect a lot from each student, but those expectations are both challenging and realistic. This means they hold all students to high standards, and they know how to meet the different needs of each individual.

As a principal, I did not want to see my kids end up in prison because we had not prepared them to function successfully in society. I knew that being able to read on grade level would provide the most solid foundation for helping them meet the demands they would face in life. All students need to receive quality literacy education that goes beyond merely preparing students for a test. Reading and writing skills are essential for students to succeed in society, and educators need to help all students read and write critically. Becoming a literate individual must be seen as a civil right, thus reading and writing skills must continually be emphasized. Research has proven that regular reading makes you a better reader, writer, speaker, listener, and thinker, so developing regular reading habits is essential. Regular reading sharpens your mind and leads to school and job success.

According to research by Clemmitt (2008), there is currently a decline in reading among the younger generations. In fact, there is less reading among younger generations, while their time using electronic media increases. The average amount of time students spend reading is declining, as is their likelihood of utilizing public library services. Research has noticed a decline in the habit of regular reading and in the reading ability of students. There is a growing gap between high-achieving readers and low-achieving readers.

Currently, society is shifting towards an online literacy, where blogs, emails, and websites are the basic locations for reading and writing. While it is important for students to develop important technological skills, research has shown that reading online is not as effective at developing key reading skills as reading novels or other print sources. Students spend less time reflecting on what is read when they read online and often only skim the articles. This is negatively impacting comprehension and vocabulary acquisition.

Clemmitt (2008) stated while our education system is currently placing a large amount of importance on literacy and reading, our society appears to be placing less emphasis on reading outside of the classroom. This is negatively impacting the literacy of our students and educators need to find a way to encourage the reading of books and discourage over-usage of online or electronic media.

As a former Reading Recovery teacher, I believe "literacy is a civil right," and that educators must accept the challenge to ensure all children are able to read on grade level. I am also aware of research indicating that the challenge for educators in urban settings is even greater. According to Gately, "Now add to that the 'cradle-to-prison pipeline, the 'poverty-to-prison' pipeline, and the 'prison-to-poverty' pipeline," (Gately, 2014). It is no secret that children born into poverty and children of color (who are disproportionately born poor) have higher rates of school failure and higher rates of incarceration than do their white and more affluent peers. Today, according to the National Center for Education Statistics, the majority of public school students are students of color, and more than half qualify for subsidized meals because of low family income. This means that more of our students face these known risk factors, so the urgency is even more pronounced today.

I fear that some recent research highlighting the role of poverty over the role of schools in this phenomenon may be doing a disservice to this and future generations of children by helping to exonerate failing school systems of their responsibility. The school system is the one institution that has the most power to change the trajectory for poor students.

The School-to–Prison Pipeline, as described in the American School Journal (2007), asserts, "What happens in schools or fails to happen determines, in large part, whether young people enter the criminal justice system." Students of color and low socioeconomic status are disproportionately represented in the criminal justice system and this is in large part due to the education they have received. In fact, many prisons plan for their future populations by looking at third grade reading standardized test scores. If children do not know how to read by third grade, they are put at a disadvantage and continually go on "losing streaks" within the educational system. Most commonly the students who do not receive adequate literacy education are those students of color or low socioeconomic status, and it is these students who need the most assistance. As written by Winn and Behizadeh (2011), "Low-quality literacy education is a key component of the school-to-prison pipeline."

I was working in an urban school district where the "school-to-prison pipeline" was all too real. I did not have to read about it in the news, I was daily confronted with the reality of a failing school system that was pushing large numbers of at-risk youth— particularly children of color—out of classrooms and into the juvenile justice system. I could see how the policies and practices that contribute to this trend became a pipeline with many entry points, from under-resourced K-12 public schools, to the over-use of zero-tolerance suspensions and expulsions and to the explosion of policing and arrests in public schools. The confluence of these practices threatens to prepare an entire generation of children for a future of incarceration.

This book is about how do we get all children not only to read, but become life-long readers. This is not just a black, white, or brown issue. It is not just a poverty issue or even just a school issue. This is an American issue that will take all of us to solve! While the news about reading failure is almost overwhelming, straightforward information about reading can provide guidance and hope. Ultimately, the solution to the literacy crisis will require principals, students, teachers, parents, policy-makers, and communities to work together towards the goal of literacy for all students. I have learned that there is no "magic bullet" or short-cut…there is only the hard work of rallying everyone with a stake in our country's future to change the trajectory!

In my school, I saw the promise of what can happen when everyone does decide to come together around the goal of ensuring literacy for all. By picking up this book, I hope you are inspired to become a proactive part of the team, ready to help your child read and succeed! I am committed and dedicated to the idea that all children can read and will read well.

This is my quest; this is my hope; this is my dream!

*"Once you learn to read you will be forever free."*
*--Frederick Douglass*

## Chapter 2

## *Changing the Trajectory of the School-to-Prison Pipeline*

Literacy is a student's lifeline to opportunity. Fundamental to literacy is becoming a thoughtful and skillful reader. Developing proficient, fluent readers requires proven instructional strategies for assessing students' current performance, honing their decoding skills to the point of automaticity, and teaching them to acquire and apply meaning from text—all within a language-rich environment that promotes higher-order thinking (Day-Bullmaster, 2014).

Millions of capable children are not learning to read well in American public, private and home schools today. The causes and cures are well known in the research community, but classroom practice has been slow to change. Because reading is critical for success in school and in the workplace, the reality of reading failure is alarming, especially to educators, policy-makers, and parents. It is critical to understand why some children fail to learn to read with the instructional methods often used today. While there are many reasons why too many children fail to develop literacy skills, there is one circumstance that has been a reliable and devastating predictor that this is likely to happen - *poverty*. Living in poverty was, and still is, the reality for virtually all of the students in my school.

Research conducted by Economic and Social Inclusion Corporation (2008) explained poverty is about not having enough money to meet basic needs including food, clothing and shelter. However, poverty is more, much more than just not having enough money. Poverty is hunger. Poverty is lack of shelter. Poverty is being sick and not being able to see a doctor. Poverty is not having access to effective schools and not knowing how to read. Poverty is not having a job, fear for the future, living one day at a time. Poverty has many faces, changing from place to place and across time. Most often, poverty is a situation people want to escape. So poverty is a call to action for the poor and the wealthy alike, a call to change the world so that many more people may have enough food to eat, adequate shelter, access to education and health, protection from violence, and a voice in what happens in their communities. In addition to a lack of money, poverty is about not being able to participate in recreational activities, not being able to send children on a day trip with their schoolmates or to a birthday party; not being able to pay for medications for an illness. People who are barely able to pay for food and shelter simply can't consider these other expenses. When people are excluded within a society, when they are not well educated and when they have a higher incidence of illness, there are negative consequences for society. The increased cost on the health system, the justice system and other systems that provide supports to those living in poverty have an impact on our economy. There is no one cause of poverty, and the results of it are different in every case. Poverty varies considerably depending on the situation. Despite the many definitions, one thing is certain; poverty is a complex societal issue. No matter how poverty is defined, it can be agreed that it is an issue that requires everyone's attention. It is important that all members of our society work together to provide the opportunities for all to reach their full potential. It helps all of us to help one another.

As a principal, the number one issue our students faced related to poverty was coming to school every day not having the tools they needed for learning. For example, often they did not bring such basic school supplies as composition books, loose-leaf paper, notebooks, zip drive, USB drives, book bags, backpacks, scissors, pencils, pencil sharpeners, ink pens, crayons, washable markers, erasers, glue markers, calculators, or computers. Children in poverty are often less likely to be read to or spoken to regularly or to have access to books, literacy-rich environments, high-quality early care, and prekindergarten programs. So, they tend to begin school already far behind. The ugly truth is that when students come to school without basic supplies and without having had prior preparation and learning experiences that are common for students from more affluent families, it can convey a message to the educator that these students are not serious about their learning.

There are numerous issues our students faced related to poverty: Living in overcrowded, substandard housing or unsafe neighborhoods; enduring community or domestic violence, separation or divorce, or the loss of family members; and experiencing financial strain, forced mobility, or material deprivation. For example, in any given year, more than half of poor children deal with evictions, utility disconnections, overcrowding, or lack of a stove or refrigerator, lack of proper supervision, physical neglect or abuse, inadequate day care and schools, unhealthy friendships and vulnerability.

Abuse is yet another major stressor for far too many children raised in poverty. Caregivers' disciplinary strategies tend to grow harsher as income decreases. Lower-income parents, on the average, are more authoritarian with their children, tending to issue harsh demands and inflict physical punishment such as spanking. Abuse occurs with much higher frequency when the parents use alcohol or drugs, and experience other stressful life events, which may lead to physical neglect of the children in those households. Poverty lives in an environment where the rate of discouraging words is higher than the rate of encouraging words. Parents, guardians, or caregivers may be stressed from their own experiences from poverty or abuse. These same caregivers may be short with their children because of their own mental health issues, working multiple jobs, and having too little time for their own stress relief, let alone quality time with their children. The students come to school each day trying to pretend they are fine. They come to school yearning to be heard and known.

Yadezra V' Shulamit (2017) stated poverty translates into *STRESS*. We all know what stress feels like. At home, at work, at school, it's that feeling that we are losing control resulting from a situation or relationship that is adverse or negative. Our bodies are hardwired to deal with stress in one of two ways: Fight or flight, a commonly referred to term, is how the body physiologically responds when under stress. The choice to stay and deal with the threat verses the choice to run to safety, is a process which the body's nervous system activates instantaneously in situations which trigger serious threat. Stress is a threat that, on occasion, is a positive thing. It can be a motivator or a resilience builder. It can give you that extra boost of energy to increase your performance or it can trigger a reaction to dangerous situations. But prolonged stress, what is commonly known as chronic (as opposed acute) stress, is detrimental to emotional, physical, and social well-being. These chronic stressors subsequently affect behavior, as symptoms begin to compromise the body. Poverty is a chronic stressor. The stress of poverty on a child in school is well documented.

Here are five, out of many, reasons why poverty affects both behavior and cognitive functioning in an academic setting:

1. Prolonged stress affects the ability of the immune system to function adequately. Weakened immune systems compromise the body's mode of defense. Children with low immune system function tend to get sick more often, having more tardiness and absences than their middle to higher class peers. Being late or absent results in missed material and added stress of making up work.

2. Parents of children in low-come families have a significantly higher rate of stress. People living on low incomes tend to be materially disadvantaged, worrying about necessities to ensure survival (food, shelter, clothing). Parents have less money to spend on recreation, social activities, vacation, leaving no time for de-stressing. Nature leaves these children exposed to an environment of stress and understandably so, such stress

becomes integrated into these children's personalities and behaviors.

3. Poor children are exposed to substandard environmental conditions, poor housing, poor neighborhood sanitation or maintenance, increased levels of crime, water or air pollution. These adverse conditions often correlate with risky decision-making amongst teens, causing the rate of delinquency and exposure to additional stress to be increased.

4. Research has proven time and time again that positive parenting improves academic achievement. Unfortunately, the opposite is true. Parents struggling to make ends meet often work in low-income jobs, being out of the home on shift work, at times when children are home. Parents return home exhausted, having less patience or energy to devote to their child's emotional needs. Positive attention is often neglected and quality relationship building, like set dinner time, homework help, or behavior modeling, fall between the cracks.

5. As with many other boundaries, children in low-income families, tend to have poor sleep. This is characterized by

shorter duration of sleep, more variability in sleep time, poorer sleeping conditions, and subsequently, higher sleep disorders. Lower academic achievement is an obvious consequence cognition memory, analytical skills are all impaired when patterns of poor sleep are established, and unfortunately, these patterns endure through childhood to adulthood (www.yadezra.net).

It is important to understand the impact poverty has on children's success. Eric Jensen's book *Teaching with Poverty in Mind* (2009) provides some powerful insights for educators as they strive to work effectively. The following excerpts offer some important background information regarding various types of poverty and some specific risk factors faced by economically disadvantaged students:

*[Poverty is defined as] "Persons with income less than that deemed sufficient to purchase basic needs such as food, shelter, clothing and other essentials are designated as poor." There are six types of poverty: situational, generational, absolute, relative, urban, and rural:*

- *Situational Poverty is generally caused by a sudden crisis or loss and is often temporary. Events causing situational poverty include environmental disasters, divorce, or severe health problems.*

- *Generational Poverty occurs in families where at least two generations have been born into poverty. Families living in this type of poverty are not equipped with the tools to move out of their situations.*

- *Absolute Poverty, which is rare in the United States, involves a scarcity of such necessity as shelter, running water, and food. Families who live in absolute poverty tend to focus on day-to-day survival.*

- *Relative Poverty refers to the economic status of a family whose income is insufficient to meet its society's average standard of living.*

- *Urban Poverty occurs in metropolitan areas with populations of at least 50,000 people. The urban poor deal with a complex aggregate of chronic and acute stressors, including crowding, violence, and noise and are dependent on often inadequate, large city services.*

- *Rural Poverty occurs in nonmetropolitan areas with populations below 50,000. In rural areas, there are more single-guardian households, and families often have less access to services, support for disabilities, and quality education opportunities.*

**The Effects of Poverty**

*Poverty involves a complex array of risk factors that adversely affect the population in a multitude of ways. The four primary risk factors afflicting families living in poverty are:*

- *Emotional and social challenges*
- *Acute and chronic stressors*
- *Cognitive lags*
- *Health and safety issues*

*Garber and Brooks-Gunn (1995) estimated that in 1995, 35 percent of poor families experienced six or more risk factors, such as divorce, sickness, or eviction. Only two-percent experienced no risk factors. In contrast, only five-percent of well-off families experienced six or more risk factors and 19 percent experienced none (Jensen, 2009).*

**The School-to-Prison Pipeline—How Discipline Systems Exacerbate the Problem**

Millions of U.S. public school students in grades K-12 are suspended or expelled in an academic school year, particularly students in middle and high school. The Civil Rights Project (2012) indicates that "when students are removed from the classroom as a disciplinary measure, the odds increase dramatically that they will repeat a grade, drop out, or become involved in the juvenile justice system." These negative consequences disproportionately affect children of color as well as students with special needs. Policymakers and practitioners urgently need to identify strategies for effectively managing students' behavior and aligning school policies in order to support student engagement and learning to reduce poor academic outcomes and juvenile justice contact. Although some state and local governments have taken promising steps to address these issues, decision makers and front-line practitioners lack a comprehensive, multisystem approach to making school discipline more effective.

    The school-to-prison pipeline starts, and thus is best avoided, in the classroom. When combined with zero-tolerance policies, a teacher's decision to refer students for punishment can mean they are pushed out of the classroom and are much more likely to be introduced into the criminal justice system. For too many urban children, entering a classroom is the first step toward ending up in a prison cell. Often, trouble in school leads to trouble with the law. A first step in changing the trajectory for these students is to create awareness within the community about discipline systems and discrimination in schools that are funneling youth of color out of schools and into the criminal justice system at rates disproportionate to their white and more affluent counterparts. We need to understand that when students of color, students of poverty and/or students with disabilities are referred for inappropriate behavior in school, they tend to meet with harsher, more frequent disciplinary actions and have a greater likelihood of finding themselves caught up in the criminal justice system as they grow up, which is known as the "school-to-prison pipeline."

Matthew Lynch's 2015 article entitled, *5 Facts Everyone Needs to Know about the School-to-Prison Pipeline* provides some startling statistics and information that I found compelling. An excerpt from this article appears below:

> *Our nation's public schools play an integral role in fostering talents. They also play a role in building our children's internal worth. It is therefore not surprising that our schools can assist in reducing our nation's prison population as well. Here are five facts everyone should know about the school-to-prison pipeline, and how to end it:*
>
> 1. *An increased prison population costs us all money. Those of us who fall outside the group of perceived misfits who make our nation's prison population may wonder why the school-to-prison pipeline should matter. Aside from caring*

*about the quality of life for other individuals, there are more tangible issues that arise from this. Each federal prisoner costs taxpayers $28,284 per year, which is about $77 per day.*

*And that's just the measurable cost. What isn't measurable is the indirect impact those incarcerations have on the economy in terms of those prisoners not contributing to the work force.*

2. *There is a link between dropping out of high school and going to prison. Sadly, over half of black young men who attend urban high schools do not earn a diploma. Of the dropouts, nearly 60 percent will go to prison at some point. There are also some eerily similar statistics for young Latino men.*

*In his piece "A Broken Windows Approach to Education Reform," Forbes writer James Marshall Crotty makes a direct connection between drop-out and crime rates. He argues that if educators will simply take a highly organized approach to keeping kids in school, it will make a difference in the crime statistics of the future. He says:*

*"Most importantly, instead of merely insisting on Common Core Standards of excellence, we must*

*provide serious sticks for non-compliance. And not just docking teacher and administrative pay. The real change needs to happen on the student and parent level."*

*He cites the effectiveness of states not extending driving privileges to high school dropouts or not allowing athletic activities for students who fail a class. With higher stakes associated with academic success, students will have more to lose if they walk away from their K-12 education. And the higher the education level, the lower the risk of criminal activity, statistically speaking.*

3. *Black and Latino men get the short end of the stick as far as this phenomenon is concerned. Aside from the dropout statistics mentioned before, an estimated 40 percent of all students that are expelled from U.S. schools are black. This leaves black students over three times more likely to face suspension than their white peers. When you add in Latino numbers, 70 percent of all in-school arrests are black or Latino students.*

*If you want to see the correlation between these school-age statistics and lifetime numbers, consider this: 61 percent of the incarcerated population are Black or Latino - despite the fact that these groups only represent 30 percent of the U.S. population. Nearly 68 percent of all men in federal prison never earned a high school diploma. The fact that the U.S. has the highest incarceration rate in the world is no surprise and the road to lockup starts in the school systems.*

4. *Expectations influence student achievement and behavior. Though all people have genetic predispositions, it is ultimately the environment that encompasses the formative years that shapes lives.*

5. *The current way of dealing with problem students is not working. When one student is causing a classroom disruption, the traditional way to address the issue has been removal -- whether the removal is for five minutes, five days or permanently. Separating the "good" students and the "bad" ones has always seemed the fair, judicious approach. On an individual level, this form of discipline may seem necessary to preserve the educational experience for others.*

*If all children came from homes that implemented a cause-and-effect approach to discipline, this might be the right answer. Unfortunately, an increasing number of students come from broken homes, or ones where parents have not the desire or time to discipline. For these students, removal from education is simply another form of abandonment and leads to the phenomenon called the "school to prison pipeline."*

As I stated before, I did not want my school to be part of a pipeline to prison for any child. I knew from experience that the first step in addressing the literacy gap for children in poverty is to build relationships with their parents by empowering them to make a positive difference for their children's future. I also knew that I needed to work with my teachers to build their capacity as culturally-responsive educators so that they would both understand their students better and would effectively manage the classroom to maximize learning.

The next chapter tells the story of my school, and how we brought a community together to address all of the obstacles that were keeping our students from realizing their full potential. We were determined to "beat the odds" for our kids!

*"The more that you read, the more things you know. The more you learn, the more places you'll go."  --Dr. Seuss*

# Chapter 3

## *The Journey to Reading Proficiency: One School's Story*

"What can we do to improve literacy in our school?" This is a question I asked myself every day and one that I expected my teachers to reflect upon. I don't claim to have all the answers, but I have spent the bulk of my career trying to find those answers. In the process, I believe I have learned some important lessons that are worth sharing. The things we did at my school made a positive impact, and I hope by sharing our story, other schools may find some measure of success as well.

In the fall of 2011, I became principal of a struggling elementary school in an urban public school district in the midwestern United States. The mission of the school was to, "Educate all students to their fullest potential, helping them to grow in academic achievement, increased English proficiency, and good moral and ethical behavior." The vision of the school was, "To promote collaboration among staff, parents, and students to achieve academic excellence. We strive to create a safe environment, which fosters the development of responsible, caring students who are lifelong learners that are prepared to meet the challenges of a culturally diverse society."

The diversity in the school was unique because many different cultures were represented. We had a significant population of Bosnian refugees, Hispanic, Vietnamese, and African-American students. Their parents spoke 16 different languages including Albanian, Pashtu, Russian, Vietnamese, Spanish, etc. Our motto was "Many Cultures, One World". This was a wonderful, diverse community that nurtured children and wanted to provide an excellent education. When I became principal, I was troubled because the test scores were low and too many students were not reading at grade level. Most of my students lived in poverty and lacked many of the background experiences that their more affluent peers enjoyed.

On my first day of school around 10:30 a.m., I walked into the main office and 10 students were sitting in chairs talking loudly, laughing and having fun, like they were at a circus. I asked the secretary why the students were sitting in the office. She stated, "The teacher put them out of the classroom and told them to go to the office." I was thinking, "How are we going to make up the students' lost instructional time?" I knew we had a problem....there was a disconnect between what my students needed from our school and my teachers' abilities to provide this support for them. I thought about my teachers' attitudes and realized that, more often than not, teachers are not adequately trained to work with children living in poverty. Working with poverty-stricken children requires teachers to be involved in every aspect of their lives, both academic and personal. Due to the lack of experience with poverty, teachers often fail to acknowledge the influence that this can have on academic achievement. Students who are living in poverty are not always given the foundation they need to achieve in school; they often have ineffective study habits and a low level of self-discipline.

I truly believed that there is no reason why schools cannot compete with Disneyland for the title, "The Happiest Place on Earth". Educators play a vital role in developing an environment that is conducive to learning, resulting in students who are competent, confident and compassionate. The most important component of a healthy learning environment is the attitude of the staff and their focus on developing positive relationships with students. Dr. Rita Pierson shared in her TED Talk, "Kids don't learn from people they don't like." From the secretary, to the custodians, counselors, teachers, and the administrative team, the attitude of the whole staff will make or break a school.

I escorted each of the 10 students back to their respective classrooms. I shared with their teachers that the superintendent expected me to be in the classrooms 80 percent of the time. As such, it was imperative that they take back their authority in the classroom by dealing with most routine discipline situations themselves. I explained that if they sent students to me, they would be giving up their power and the behavior would continue as soon as they returned to the classroom. I also explained that having students out of the classroom disrupted the learning for them as well as for the other students. At first, the teachers were not happy with my approach to discipline, but eventually, they would come to understand the big pay-off. I knew I had to help them understand the importance of taking a very different approach to discipline that was built on a foundation of positive relationships with their students.

When I became principal of the school, I noticed that teachers' attitudes toward students and parents of poverty was genuinely caring and respectful for most students, however I realized right away that many simply did not know how to effectively manage their classrooms. Some of the teachers were fearful of the students and parents and had no clue of what growing up in poverty was like. They were often shocked to learn about what typically goes on and doesn't go on in the homes of their students. The majority of teachers tried to create an environment of mutual respect and rapport, but at times the teachers' interactions with at least some students was negative, demeaning, sarcastic, inappropriate or indifferent. In response, some students' interactions were characterized by conflict, sarcasm or put-down. Some teachers did not establish a culture for learning but communicated the importance of content with little conviction, and conveyed low expectations for student achievement. Some teachers struggled with managing classroom procedures, management of instructional groups, and performance of non-instructional duties resulting in loss of instructional time. Many instructional groups were off task and not productively engaged in the learning. A lot of instructional time was lost managing student behavior. Too often, no standards of conduct appeared to have been established, or students were confused as to what the standards were. The teachers attempted to manage student misbehavior but with uneven results.

My first year as a principal at the school was very challenging working with poverty students. A third grade female student was sent to the office literally every day for being disrespectful and disrupting the classroom environment. I would conference with the student and one day, I asked her, "Why are you being put out of the classroom every day?" The student stated, "Dr. Morrow you don't understand. Our electric is turned off and I need to get a job to help my mom with the household bills." I could not believe a third grade student was talking about getting a job to help her mother with the household bills. A third grade student should not have to worry about having a job or paying bills. As a reflective practitioner, I wrote daily in my journal to reflect on my practice and my problem solving skills. As I was writing about this student, I began to cry thinking about when I was in the third grade that having to help with household bills would have been the farthest thing from my mind. I realized at that moment, that I was "out of touch" with reality my students faced each and every day. Although I had spent my entire career working in schools with disadvantaged students, it still hadn't "hit me" until that child shared her worries with me. It was clear to me that she would not be able to focus while she was worrying about what situation she might face when she returned home each day.

Today, students come to school with so much baggage on their minds they often can't focus due to their home environment. I decided to share this story with the staff at the monthly staff meeting to help them better understand and begin to empathize with our students. If I had not taken time out of my busy schedule to truly listen to the student, I'm sure she would have continued disrupting the classroom environment. From that day forward, I visited her classroom everyday first thing in the morning to make sure she was at school, that she had breakfast, and something to take home to eat later that evening. I also conferenced with the child's mom to address the concerns and find ways to support this family so that her child could be relieved of adult responsibilities. This experience, more powerfully than any other, convinced me that principals and teachers must have close relationships with students to help them to know that someone cares about them and will find ways to support them. Students will rise to meet your expectations if they have a relationship with you and they believe you truly care about them.

This experience, combined with the situation of the "first day office visitors" helped me to form a plan of action to move the school in a more positive direction. As an instructional leader, I decided to implement the 80/20 rule as one of the most helpful concepts for life and time management. Also known as the Pareto Principle, this rule suggests that 20 percent of your activities will account for 80 percent of your results. For me, this meant that I set a firm schedule for myself spending 80 percent of my time observing teaching and learning in the classroom and providing immediate feedback to my teachers. This meant that I was not sitting in my office just waiting to "babysit" disruptive students. It took some time to change the culture that had emerged prior to me coming to the building, but through consistent practice and teamwork, teachers did begin to reclaim their authority within their own classrooms. The struggle was well worth it and allowed me to see what level of learning was happening in the school each day.

Another important part of changing the school culture was the implementation of the "I'm Going to College" initiative. We had to get our students to begin to envision a different future for themselves. Many came from backgrounds where none of their family had gone to college or even considered doing so. We knew that we had to build awareness of the possibilities and plant seeds of self-confidence and personal goal-setting. If our students didn't see college and career as real possibilities for themselves, they knew they were stuck. Each classroom adopted a college or university and made that school an aspiration school for the class. Teachers displayed school pennants, we supplied school tee-shirts, students conducted research about their school, etc. We even held school assemblies were invited college recruiters, parents and community members to come and talk to students about college life. Teachers wore their academic regalia, and recruiters distributed information and swag to the students. All of this was done in an effort to make "college not just the dream, but the plan" for our students.

Much more challenging than getting students to believe in themselves was the challenge of changing teachers' mental models about what students could do. The goal of one of my first professional development sessions was to have a courageous conversation about race. I opened the session by displaying a graphic organizer designed to capture their perceptions about students in the following categories:

| African-American | White | Hispanic | Special Needs | ELL |
|---|---|---|---|---|
| • Protective of families/ siblings<br>• Confrontational<br>• Not motivated<br>• Don't want to work<br>• Antagonistic<br>• Challenging<br>• Hopeful<br>• Less-structured<br>• Need a lot of emotional support | • Silly<br>• Playful<br>• Lazy<br>• Teacherpleasers<br>• Boring<br>• Less needy | • Friendly<br>• Not risk-takers<br>• Easy to get along with<br>• Like school<br>• Pile lots of people in a small house | • Slow<br>• Don't try<br>• Easily frustrated<br>• Cry easily | • Cooperative<br>• Friendly<br>• Hard workers<br>• Prepared to learn<br>• Compliant |

I asked each teacher to write their perceptions for each group on a separate sticky note and place the sticky note onto the graphic organizer. When we had finished, I was speechless! It was hard for me to believe that my colleagues felt this way about students and that they were the people teaching our kids. The negative mental models that teachers had about kids, particularly African-American kids, made me question whether or not I would be able to work with this group of teachers. Did I have the skill set to move this school forward? Would the teachers be able to change their mental models? Would they be able to develop a growth mindset? Would they be able to reflect on their own practice? Would they ever believe that all kids can learn and achieve at high levels? I knew I had my work cut out for me, but I'm not the kind of person to shrink from hard work! I dug in deeper!

As a principal, I knew I had to combat negative beliefs and attitudes about children. Although the descriptors of African-American students tended to be much more negative, the descriptors of the different groups in our school were generally negative. I decided to approach this concern by focusing on what we believe about kids from poverty as this was the one common dominator that seemed to color the perceptions of all our students in such a negative light. We made it a standing agenda item on our monthly staff meetings to discuss the symptoms of poverty that show up in the classrooms and how best to address those symptoms. The teachers collaborated about the various behaviors not conducive to learning, such as students' angry outbursts, difficulty concentrating, irritability, agitation, social withdrawal, and emotional numbness. We also discussed how chronic absenteeism, chronic health issues, sleeplessness, separation anxiety, obesity, and poor nutrition, depression, sleep disorders, eating disorders are clues for educators to use in evaluating whether a student is experiencing the stress of poverty or if he/she might be a victim of trauma. After listening to the teachers complain about the students' negative behavior, I knew I had to think outside the box to get them to believe that students who live in poverty can learn and they will rise to your expectations.

We collaborated at the monthly staff meetings about the impact of poverty and trauma on learning and how to address and remove barriers in the lives of our students. Because teachers work so closely with students who carry within them the physical and emotional pain and scars of poverty and trauma, these teachers are at risk of burnout. This burnout comes from students passing on their pain and stress to the teachers, administrators, and staff. Without knowledge, skills, and strategies to minimize this impact, educators' physical and mental health will be affected, increasing absenteeism, and contributing to them leaving the profession. The weariness that educators experience is not just from the amount of work and hours they perform, it comes from the circumstances in which they teach and the emotional investment they make in their students' lives.

Turnover among educators and staff at high-poverty schools is significant because of the burnout that results from working with students carrying the pain of poverty and trauma in their lives. This turnover perpetuates the cycle of poverty. Schools that do not retain the same quality principals for at least five to eight years in a row do not realize the full gifts of those administrators. Leadership circles have known for years that it takes five to eight years for a leader to hit a stride with their gifts, talents, and understanding of the culture and needs of their organization. Schools and their principals are also at risk when they focus on less than a comprehensive approach to education, focusing solely on a curriculum and assessments that measure the attempts to teach to it.

To help teachers cope with stress management, I invited a consultant from the Mental Health of America of Eastern Missouri to our monthly staff meetings to help us manage stress on the job. The consultant provided professional development workshops that consisted of the following:

- What is Stress?
- What Causes Stress?
- Good Stress Versus Bad Stress
- Managing Stress on the Job
- Common Sources of Stress
- How Stress Affects Us At Work
- How Stress Affects Our Health and Wellness
- Strategies for Managing Stress
- Stress: Coping with Everyday Problems
- Stress: Managing Life's Pressures
- Stress: Stress and Mental Illness
- Stress: Stress Assessment Checklist

- Burnout Assessment Tool
- Burnout Prevention

It is my belief that this intervention helped us focus on taking care of ourselves and our team members, so the stress from our students' poverty and trauma could not interfere with our performances in the classroom. Focusing on our own mental health helped us improve student performance, as well as our own performance. I feel this was the key ingredient to helping us achieve Adequate Yearly Progress (AYP) on the Missouri Assessment Program (MAP) test.

There were many times as a principal, I often wanted to ask my colleagues, "Why did you become a teacher?" Some of us chose the teaching profession because we love children, we want to make a difference in the lives of students, and we want to improve the world. The majority of the teachers wanted to be a "Champion for Kids" so I decided to build on this foundational set of beliefs that we tended to share to take the next steps forward in improving our school's effectiveness. I knew that to have a strong culture and "buy-in" from my teachers, I needed to find a way for us to collaborate on a regular basis. We decided to implement the Professional Learning Community (PLC) model as the vehicle to accomplish this goal. PLCs are a group of educators that meets regularly, shares expertise, and works collaboratively to improve teaching skills and the academic performance of students.

We first had to agree that we believed all students can learn. Then we could use the "four critical corollary questions" of PLCs to drive our conversations. Those questions, as anyone familiar with PLCs knows are:

- What do we expect our students to learn? (Goals/Expectations)
- How will we know they are learning? (Assessment)
- How will we respond when they don't learn? (Intervention)
- How will we respond if they already know it? (Gifted)

We began meeting weekly in grade level PLC teams to collaborate, review data from student assessments, and discuss strategies to improve instruction. The data from these exercises showed that our students had a relative strength in mathematics and a severe deficit in English-Language Arts (ELA), so we decided to attack the weakest area first. I knew with my background in Reading Recovery, that I use could this area as a vehicle to train teachers and begin changing mindsets. My first order of business was to determine how best to prepare my teachers to meet the needs of a broader range of students than I had ever encountered before. The student population was quite diverse, with a high percentage (40 percent) being English Language Learners (ELL). All of the students (100 percent) were eligible for free/reduced lunch, and fewer than 10 percent were reading at grade level. The needs were simply too great to expect regular classroom teachers alone to address. Many students, for example, required at least three or four times as much instruction as the average student in order to achieve normal progress in learning to read. In many classrooms, the number of students requiring this amount of additional instruction approached 5-75 percent of the class. The regular classroom simply did not have the time or resources to provide the required amount of instruction within the school day for most struggling students.

I spent the first year working to get the staff on board, providing training on the Five Essential Components of Reading and implemented the Readers are Leaders initiative for students. We also established PLCs as a framework to improve student achievement and overall school success. We began to examine our data around the four essential questions of the PLC, i.e. "What do we want students to learn? How will we know they have learned? What will we do when they have not learned? What will we do when they have already learned?"

The next year, we turned a focus toward generating solid parent and community support. We first conducted the

Elementary Reading Attitude Survey that asked parents to provide information about their children's reading habits and interests as well as the parents' reading levels, attitudes, and willingness/ability to support their children's reading. We used this information to create the Reading is My Game initiative. This initiative consisted of several components including the Parent Reading Contract, The Reading Oath, Parent Wall of Fame, and Parents Make a Difference.

This initiative was one of the most successful and powerful things we did to motivate our students to read. There were two walls in the hallway, one for parents and one for students. STAR readers, i.e. students reading above and on grade level, were posted on one wall. The names of parents whose children were reading above or on grade level were posted on another wall outside the office. When parents visited the school, they always looked for their child's and their names on the wall. When they did not see their child's name posted, they would ask why and how that could be changed? We told them that their child needed to demonstrate reading skills at grade level or above. This really seemed to motivate parents to work more closely with their children. It was a simple thing, but the impact was incredible!

The Reading Oath was another part of the initiative to help students connect to the importance of reading. Students recited this oath every day in the morning after the Pledge of Allegiance. **Let this oath inspire your students to become lifelong readers!**

*I promise to read*
*Each day and each night.*
*I know it's the key*
*To growing up right.*

*I'll read to myself,*
*I'll read to a crowd.*
*It makes no difference*
*If silent or loud.*

*I'll read at my desk,*
*At home and at school,*
*On my bean bag or bed,*
*By the fire or pool.*

*Each book that I read*
*Puts smarts in my head,*
*'Cause brains grow more thoughts*
*The more they are fed.*

*So I take this oath*
*To make reading my way*
*Of feeding my brain*
*What it needs every day.*

           --Debra Angstead, Missouri-NEA

We began to celebrate every achievement and even the promise of achievement! Every morning, about 20 moms and dads would stand against the wall in the gym, watching me lead the daily rally to boost excitement about the importance of reading on grade level. I would shout, "Happy Monday! It is very important that every student can read and perform on grade level. Raise your hand if you read a book for 30-minutes last night. Be honest!" Then, I would call on different students to come to the microphone to do a BOOK TALK. The students would clap for each other and praise each other for sharing their book talk.

During the morning rally, I would recognize students for a number of accomplishments. These included being Caught in the Act of Reading, Perfect Attendance, 90/90 Attendance, STAR Reading Assessment, Reading Above Grade Level, Reading On Grade Level, and Making Progress. In addition to the daily recognitions, the school held a number of other activities to support literacy. These included Drop Everything and Read (DEAR) Time, Weekly Reading Logs, College Day, Spirit Day, Monthly Literacy Themes, College and Career Readiness Recruiters, College Fair, Community Workers, Kids' Voting Campaign, Red Apple Award for Staff, Grade Level Competitions, and Hoop It Up For Reading (Staff vs Students).

For me as the principal, one of the most important indications that we were on the right track was that teachers began talking about the growth they were seeing in their students.

When students brought back their reading logs indicating they were reading at home at least 30-minutes each night, working on high frequency words, building comprehension, and reading grade-level texts, teachers began to notice a difference in student performance in school. Seeing results is one of the most powerful ways to change minds, and this was happening before my eyes! I could actually see the culture shifting in our school!

    The shift was happening, but it wasn't fast enough to avert negative attention from the state. During my second year as principal, the school qualified and was awarded a School Improvement Grant (SIG) to support focused school improvement efforts. The aim of school turnaround is to improve student outcomes by changing how schools and classrooms operate. School turnaround demands quick, dramatic improvement within three years. In school turnaround, a leader must quickly identify and train one or two key staff members who are already qualified and prepared to initiate shared leadership. School turnaround literature builds on effective school-wide practices but focuses on how to speed up and increase the impact of these practices.

    I was considering stepping down from the principal leadership because of the negative perception of the SIG. I had to do a lot of praying and reflecting with my mentors to process the School Turnaround Model. I was always spreading the gospel about TEAMWORK MAKES THE DREAM WORK! What is a team? My definition of *team* is a group of people working together to achieve a common goal. I had to reflect and ask myself if I was really being a team player if I quit the principal leadership. I will always remember the after-school meeting with the team when I told them we would become a SIG school the following school year. The team was very upset and they had many questions such as, "Why are we becoming a SIG School when our test scores are improving each school year? How long will we be in the SIG? Can I transfer to another school?" I felt a bit like a hypocrite because of my thoughts of stepping down, but I had to stand in front of the TEAM that day and tell them that I believed we could make AYP if we stayed on track and continued working hard. I honestly believed in my heart this was the team that could win the CHAMPIONSHIP, and I told them so. My favorite quote was, "Talent wins games, but teamwork and intelligence wins championships!"

As the school's leader, now in "Turnaround", my thoughts turned to the best way to translate my own state of "data informed-ness" into meaningful action. I had come to understand that the key was to put my efforts into creating data leaders beyond the principal's office. I identified some key leaders on every PLC team to serve as data leaders. These leaders were called the *Using Data Colleagues*. These leaders were trained in the data-team process, and they led their PLCs in using the Response to Intervention (RTI) Three-Tier Framework to analyze student data. The *Using Data Colleagues* are still in every classroom in the school! Accomplishing this level of a "using data school culture" depended on a process that involved professional development, support, and dedication over time. We worked at it every day.

According to research, it takes three to seven years to "turnaround" a school. Our school had not met AYP since 2004. By engaging all stakeholders i.e. parents, teachers, students, administrators, and community members, in the process, providing intensive training and resources, and focusing on nurturing a positive school culture grounded in literacy, we finally made AYP in 2015. The school is currently fully-accredited.

---

**School Turnaround Timeline**

2011-2012: Implementation of College and Career Readiness
 "I'm Going to College" Initiative
2012-2013: Implementation of Academic Achievement
 "Readers Are Leaders"
2013-2014: Implementation of Literacy Focus
 "Reading Comprehension"
2015-2016: Implementation of "Reading Is My Game" Initiative

School turnaround requires a constant monitoring of students' academic progress through regular testing and weekly meetings among teachers who use data to adjust their instruction.

A colorful mural was placed in the school's first floor hallway to show where students fell in reading proficiency. One afternoon in October, a fifth-grader, left the computer lab after completing the monthly assessment. He learned his name would be moved to a different category on the mural. He had advanced more than one year in a matter of months. He was so excited and proud of his accomplishment. He is just one example of a child for whom the "pipeline to prison" is hopefully being broken!

*"Books make great gifts because they have whole worlds inside of them."   --Neil Gaiman*

# Chapter 4

## *Third Grade Matters: The Reading Milestone*

Reading is a fundamental skill that we all use every single day. We read newspapers, magazines, books, directions, text messages, recipes, emails, safety warnings, etc. Reading is everywhere!  It's no secret that developing proficient reading skills from a young age is essential not only for academic success, but for success in all areas and stages of life. However, reading can be a challenging skill that many students struggle to master. As educators, we want nothing more than to help our students become comfortable and confident readers.

Reading is the most important academic skill because almost 90 percent of all school work requires reading. If your child becomes a good reader, many learning and school problems can be prevented. Reading well by third grade is one of the most important predictors of high school graduation and career success. During the early school years, children are focused on learning to read. Once children hit third grade, they begin reading to learn. That means if children can't read well, they will fall behind in other subjects – science, social studies and even math, which increasingly depends on word problems as well as math facts. Without strong reading skills, children fall further and further behind – making catch-up that much harder as the years go on.

For those who truly wish to leave no child behind, the racial and poverty achievement gaps in literacy are among the most challenging issues in education today, and nowhere does this issue manifest itself more perniciously than in our schools. Recent research reveals that students who cannot read by the end of the third grade are more likely to drop out of high school and experience higher levels of poverty, crime and overall lack of success in their adult lives. Concurrently, it has been reported that 42 million adult Americans cannot read at all or have severely limited reading levels. These statistics, both staggering and parallel, make us face a simple truth: If you cannot read and write you are at a great disadvantage.

Grade-level reading is a proven indicator to the future success of America, and that is why we must place greater emphasis on providing classroom teachers with focused coaching and professional development. Currently, children who are not reading proficiently by third grade are widely seen as being in academic crisis. Educators are increasingly looking for actions they can take in the younger grades, even as early as preschool, to head off failure later in a child's school career. The stakes are clear. Studies have shown that without effective intervention, children who read significantly below grade level by third grade continue to struggle in school and eventually face a much higher likelihood of dropping out altogether. In order to address this literacy crisis, states have implemented a variety of policies intended to help identify reading problems before they become deep rooted, and then steer children into instruction that will change their trajectory. Such policies include training teachers in research-based reading interventions, connecting students with specially trained reading instructors, offering one-on-one and group instruction in reading, and providing summer school to students who need help.

## **What Does "Grade Level" Mean?**

Research by Read Charlotte (2014) explained as children progress through school, they learn the ins and outs of letters, sounds, words, and language. They put that knowledge to use by reading words, sentences, and books.

When a child is reading "on grade level" it means that he/she has mastered the skills needed to read and understand words and sentences in books at the expected level of difficulty. That could mean reading simple words (cat, hat, hop) in kindergarten, or understanding compound words (aggravating, swiped, exclaimed) in third grade.

Here are some questions parents can ask their child's teacher to find out whether or not the child is reading on grade level:

- What reading skills has my child mastered?
- What reading skills is he/she working on?
- What level book should he/she be bringing home? (Books are often leveled according to how difficult they are; A is the easiest. Check for a sticker with a letter to find the level.)
- What kinds of words should my child be able to read on his own?
- What skills does my child need to practice at home? How can I help?

Ensuring a child reads on grade level by third grade must start at home. According to Heather Grocott (2007), "Children should not only be read to as infants and toddlers, but should be able to touch, see, and explore books of their own. As children grow and develop, reading at home should be a consistent every day activity that the whole family experiences." The efforts of families must also be supported through exposure to high quality early literacy programs in preschool, daycare and elementary school settings. The importance of early literacy programs cannot be overemphasized. Irene Fountas and Gay Su Pinnell (1999) and Loretta Caravette (2011) have identified and described six critical stages of a child's literacy development. These stages are:

- *Early Literacy*
- *The Emergent Reader*
- *The Early Reader*
- *The Transitional Reader*
- *The Self-Extending Reader*
- *The Advanced Reader*

### ***Early Literacy***

*At this stage, during a child's early years (two-five years old), parents are integral to early literacy foundation. This stage is initiated by parents reading aloud to their children and involving their children in as much written and spoken language as possible. According to Caravette (2011), research shows that "reading to a child from an early age influenced performance in school for the better. During this stage in their development, children begin to develop vocabulary, sound structure, the meaning of print, the structure of stories, and language" (Caravette 2011). Children are also beginning to learn the alphabet and the corresponding letter names and sounds.*

## ***The Emergent Reader***

*Students are typically in this stage of development during their year in kindergarten. Teachers and parents utilize picture or story books and continue reading to children aloud. Children begin to develop key literacy skills for the future. Children begin to match spoken words with written words and learn to read from left to right on the page. Students are still learning the alphabet, and the letter names, shapes, and sounds. Teachers begin to teach students to write the alphabet and children begin to recognize upper and lowercase letters.*

## ***The Early Reader***

*Students often reach this stage in their literacy development in first grade. Students continue to understand the alphabet and "symbol-sounds relationships" (Caravette 2011: Fountas & Pinnell 1999). Students at this stage typically develop a set of high frequency words that they begin to use dominantly. In addition, students generally, develop greater writing skills and learn different kinds of texts including fiction, nonfiction, and poetry.*

### *The Transitional Reader*

*Students generally, enter this stage of literacy development during the second grade. At this point students are becoming more fluent readers and begin reading for meaning (Caravette 2011). Students develop their skills in the use of "meaning, grammar, letter cues, and phonics" to read more fully (Caravette 2011). Students at this stage have mastered a greater number of high frequency words and rely less on pictures when reading. Students begin to move away from picture books and towards books with more text. Tools such as the dictionary and thesaurus are introduced during this stage.*

### *The Self-Extending Reader*

*Typically by third grade, students are beginning to enter this stage of literacy development. Students are "moving from learning to read to reading to learn" (Caravette 2011). Students utilize reading in all of their other subjects and rely on reading to understand various content and applications. Students have a large core of high frequency words and can utilize their reading strategies to learn and understand unknown or new words. Students begin to understand the various purposes for reading and transition into a focus on chapter books. Students at this stage begin to connect with characters and enjoy reading books with diverse groups of characters.*

### ***The Advanced Reader***

*Students generally enter this final stage of literacy development in the fourth grade. Students continue to learn and develop all of the previously mentioned learning and reading strategies and will continue to utilize these skills throughout the rest of their lives. Students read a wide variety of texts for meaning and understanding.*

*While children and students develop as readers, it is possible for them to possess aspects of two different stages at once. Teachers and parents need to work on understanding where each child is in their development to best aid students in achieving full literacy (Fountas and Pinell, 1999; Caravette, 2011).*

Educators understand the importance of third grade as a benchmark in children's literacy development. Often, teachers tell parents, "In grades K-3, children learn to read. After that, they read to learn." While this is rather simplistic and not altogether accurate, it emphasizes the importance of the developmental milestone third grade represents. Children who find themselves reading below grade level at third grade tend to find themselves behind throughout their school careers and beyond. They may not be able to catch up and are at increased risk of dropping out, living in poverty, and/or winding up in prison. This is not only a crisis for these individual children, it is a crisis that will undoubtedly impact our nation's future stability and well-being.

*"What we have loved, others will love, and we will teach them how." --William Wordsworth*

# Chapter 5:

## *Building Our Literacy Model*

As we began to tackle the monumental task of improving literacy in our school, we had to engage in some deep research into what models, instructional strategies and/or programs would best meet the literacy instruction needs of our students. Our research took us on a journey that ultimately led us to create a plan that pulled from a variety of sources. In this chapter, I will share with you some of the research we explored, and what we finally designed for our unique situation.

**The Five Essential Components of Reading**

A high quality literacy program contains all of the components necessary for students to master reading and writing. Each component is a piece of the puzzle that when assembled together in a coherent way results in a successful literacy program. One of the first sources we explored was the work of The National Reading Panel (1997). That panel had identified five essential components in order to teach each student to become a successful reader and writer, and we wanted to ensure that our model would include all of these elements:

***Phonemic Awareness*** *– Phonemic awareness is the ability to hear, identify, and manipulate the individual sounds-phonemes in spoken words. Effective phonemic awareness instruction teaches children to notice, think about, and manipulate sounds in spoken language.*

***Phonics*** *– Phonics instruction teaches children the relationships between the letters (graphemes) of written language and the individual sounds (phonemes) of spoken language. It teaches children to use these relationships to read and write words.*

***Fluency*** *– Fluency is the ability to read a text accurately and quickly. When fluent readers read silently, they recognize words automatically. They group words quickly to help them gain meaning from what they read. Fluent readers read aloud effortlessly and with expression. Their reading sounds natural, as if they are speaking. Readers who have not yet developed fluency read slowly, word by word. Their oral reading is choppy and plodding.*

***Vocabulary*** *– Vocabulary refers to the words we must know to communicate effectively. In general, vocabulary can be described as oral vocabulary or reading vocabulary. Oral vocabulary refers to words that we use in* *speaking or recognize in listening. Reading vocabulary refers to words we recognize or use in print.*

**Comprehension** – *Comprehension is the reason for reading. If readers can read the words but do not understand what they are reading, they are not really reading. In other words, it is the process of constructing meaning from the words read. It involves the reader's prior knowledge and past experiences as well as what is written in the text* (Put Reading First, 2006).

We examined the work of Morrison, Bachman, and Connor (2005). Their work provided a framework for ensuring that whatever model we ultimately designed would be comprehensive and include the contributions of all key stakeholders. These researchers discuss seven ways to improve the state of literacy among students:

- *Start Early (before children begin school)*
- *Promote Effective Parenting*
- *Provide Uniformly High-Quality Childcare Experiences for Children*
- *Foster Children's Self-Regulation As Well As Their Literacy Skills*
- *Strive for Individualized Instruction*

- *Enhance the Quality and Status of Teachers (Morrison, et al, 2005)*

While serving as principal of the school, I was also working as an adjunct professor at a local university, teaching reading strategies to practicing teachers from a variety of school districts throughout the region. This opportunity allowed me to learn about what other districts were using. I became intrigued with the "balanced literacy" approach to literacy instruction, and we explored this framework in some depth. An overview of what we learned about this approach follows:

**Balanced Literacy Framework**

*Many balanced literacy models are composed of three major components:* **Reading Workshop**, **Writing Workshop**, *and* **Word Work**.

<u>Reading Workshop</u>

- **Shared Reading:** *During Shared Reading, teachers provide explicit comprehension instruction.*
- **Guided Reading**: *The Guided Reading lesson plans for every leveled book provide a scaffolded approach to instruction.*

- ***Independent Reading:*** *Independent Reading provides students the opportunity to apply reading strategies and skills in a text of personal interest.*

## Writing Workshop

*Writing Workshop includes opportunities for Shared Writing, Guided Writing, and Independent Writing. Writing Workshop begins with teacher-directed lessons followed by time for students to write. Teachers confer with students and guide their writing development.*

## Word Work

*The goal of working with words is to guide students to become more fluent readers and writers.*

***Phonemic Awareness and Phonics:*** *Phonemic awareness and phonics help the youngest students learn letter-sound relationships.*

***High-Frequency Words and Vocabulary:*** *Students build on a foundation of word knowledge by emphasizing word structure and vocabulary. Students extend their vocabulary in order to apply it in the context of reading (Readinga-z.com, 2018).*

Finally, we explored the Title I School Improvement Project developed by the North Dakota Department of Public Instruction. This project described a structure known as "The Daily Five." As we learned more about this structure, it became clear that we would modify and adopt this approach for use in our school. The North Dakota version of The Daily Five consists of the following components:

- *Read to Self*
- *Read to Someone*
- *Listen to Reading*
- *Work on Writing*
- *Word Work (Lienhardt, Sigmond & Cooley (1981)*

**Our Model**

We called our model the Small Group Instruction Model, and it consists of six components:

- Teacher Time
- Read to Self
- Listen to Reading
- Partner Read
- Word Work
- Writing

Teachers provide guided reading instruction with four to six students, rotating every 20 minutes.

We found that teachers in our school needed very specific guidelines and directions about how to implement our model, so we developed a Guided Reading Block Schedule that identified how much time should be devoted to each component. A sample of the schedule is provided below:

| TIME | ACTIVITY |
| --- | --- |
| 9:10-9:30 | Attendance/Lunch Count, Morning Meeting, Do Now |
| 9:30-9:45 | **Read Aloud**: Teacher models fluency, while students' listen for pleasure. |
| 9:45-10:00 | **Shared Reading**: Whole group instruction; Teacher reads passage from a story focusing on vocabulary or introduces a comprehension or phonics skill (mini lesson with anchor chart). |
| 10:00-11:00 Rotating every 20 minutes | **Small Group Instruction**: Daily 5 – A management system for reading workshop<br><br>**Teacher Time** – Guided reading/skill based activity<br>**Read to Self** – Student reads self-selected text<br>**Listen to Reading** – Listen to story on computer<br>**Partner Read** – Read with someone<br>**Word Work** – Phonics, vocabulary, consonant blends, word chunks, word families, etc.<br>**Writing** – Prompts, steps to the writing process, journal writing, etc.<br><br>Teacher provides guided reading instruction with four to six students, rotating every 20 minutes. |
| 11:00-11:30 | **Project-Based Learning – Using the Writing Process**<br>"Today a Reader, Tomorrow a Leader" |

My role was to daily monitor how the model was actually being implemented in all classrooms. When I noticed a teacher struggling, I would identify a model classroom that the struggling teacher could visit to observe and collaborate with the model classroom teacher. It was important to build an atmosphere of "safe practice" so that, in the beginning, I wasn't there to evaluate, but rather to support, coach, and encourage. My observations told me where the majority of my teachers were having difficulty so that I could tailor our professional development sessions accordingly. Over time, teachers became more and more confident and student results began to validate our efforts.

*"A house without books is like a room without windows."*
*--Heinrich Mann*

# Chapter 6
## *High Achievement Starts At Home*

Parents are often the first ones to recognize that their child is struggling too much and falling behind. Time and time again, it is the parent who sees the problem and persists with determination to get the right kind of help for the child.

Unfortunately, parents in poverty are at a definite disadvantage when it comes to recognizing the extent to which their children may be struggling, thus they may not have a sense of urgency to advocate for the school to address concerns as they arise. This phenomenon occurs for a number of reasons. Parents in poverty may be overwhelmed with the daily struggles of providing basic necessities of life, they may lack awareness/knowledge of academic expectations, and/or they may hold a belief system that assumes the professional educators should take full responsibility for their child's education.

Parents want to see their children succeed in school, whether they go to Christian, private, or public schools. When parents get involved in school, those schools improve dramatically; their children are more motivated and better behaved in the classroom; their diverse needs are met more effectively; and scores on achievement tests are significantly higher.

Students of poverty often live in chaotic and unstructured environments. They live day to day. They may be unable to manage their emotions, have poor role models, and feel they have no choice or control over their destiny. Students may be depressed, have a fear of failure due to past experiences or have acquired failure expectations from their parents.

One of the social issues facing children of poverty is emotional trauma. The lack of emotional nurturing can lead to feelings of alienation, inadequacy, depression and anxiety. There is a craving for attention and a need to belong. The characteristics that are lacking in poverty environments are those that help foster effective learning and academic success. As educators, we need to make sure students feel that they are loveable, important and acceptable human beings by making them feel secure and good about themselves by building trusting respectful relationships with them.

Developing positive relationships with parents and families of low socio-economic status and getting them involved with their children's education and school activities is a challenge. In order to address this challenge, it is first necessary to understand the dynamics of parenting in the context of poverty. Parenting is a critical process affecting many developmental outcomes for children living in poverty. Overall, parental support and involvement in school activities is lower among poor parents. Most parents, regardless of their socio-economic status, love their children and want them to achieve and be college and career ready. Many of these parents need to learn strategies that can help them cope and help their children get a chance at breaking the cycle of poverty.

Home-school collaboration is particularly important for children of poverty in helping to facilitate better educational outcomes. Because relationships with these families are often the most difficult to cultivate, teachers and schools need to make an extra effort to reach out to parents and families of poverty, helping them to help their children. The more parents participate, the better their students tend to achieve and succeed. Sometimes reaching parents can be difficult if they have no phone, do not speak English or cannot read. It is even more critical that we find ways to reach these parents. Once we do reach them, however, there is no guarantee that they will be positive, cooperative, or receptive. We must do our best to attempt to foster a positive relationship with them in the face of resistance, trying to convince them that their involvement is for the benefit of the child. Only when parents trust and feel accepted by teachers, can the teachers stand a chance of getting through to the parents.

Parents should feel welcome to observe the class and spend time helping out in the classroom, lunchroom or during activities. They should be encouraged to view student work, accomplishments and portfolios when they come to school so they can become more aware of their child's abilities and talents and can discuss them with their children in a meaningful way. Parental involvement sends a message to all children, not only the child of the involved parent, that school is important. Parental involvement can also be contagious, especially when other children observe positive interactions among the teacher, student and parent.

Teachers should keep parents informed of what is going on in the classroom and encourage parents to talk to their children about school. A monthly calendar of topics and activities can help parents to read with their children or have their children to read to them. A class trip to the local public library where every student signs up to receive a library card is a great opportunity for children to get excited about literacy.

Parental involvement is a powerful component to the success of any school improvement initiative, however in situations where poverty is a challenge, the broader community must also play a pivotal role. Home-School Community Partnerships are a powerful way to improve academic outcomes at both the elementary and secondary level. When schools, parents, families, and communities work together, students:

- Adapt well to school
- Attend school more regularly
- Complete homework more consistently
- Earn higher grades and test scores
- Graduate and go on to college
- Have better relationships with their parents
- Have higher-self-esteem

This is true for students of all ages, all backgrounds, and across race and ethnicity. Furthermore, a variety of supports cutting across the spectrum of social, health, and academic needs may be necessary for school success. High quality schools have demonstrated track records connecting with community resources in all domains of development. Schools, parents, and the community should work together to promote the health, well-being, and learning of all students. When schools actively involve parents and engage community resources they are able to respond effectively to the health-related needs of students.

Home-school community partnerships are a shared responsibility and reciprocal process whereby schools and other community agencies and organizations engage families in meaningful and culturally appropriate ways, and families take initiative to actively support their children's development and learning. Schools and community organizations also make efforts to listen to parents, support them, and ensure that they have the tools to be active partners in their children's school experience. Community partnerships are essential to help support the academic success of our students and parents.

Home-school community partnerships come in a variety of styles. Such partnerships build understanding of the education process and are beneficial to the students we serve. There is an African proverb that states, "It takes a whole village to raise a child." Partnerships allow the whole village to help educate our children.

The leadership team at my school was concerned about students' reading achievement and the degree to which students engaged in independent, out of school reading activities. In an effort to improve reading and school-home partnerships, the school began to collect data for the baseline study, using student reading logs. Data was recorded reflecting the number of books read for a period of sixteen weeks. The logs were analyzed and the researchers discovered that first graders read an average of 21 books during the 16 week period, second graders - 35 books, and third graders - 10 books. We noted a dramatic drop-off occurred with fourth graders, who reported an average of four books read over this 16 week period; fifth graders, three books. With this data as the reference point, we developed a program designed to increase the amount of independent reading. The program involved three components: a continuation of the use of student reading logs; a program forming book clubs, to encourage parents and students to increase the amount of at-home reading and encouraging everyone to set goals; and teachers using charts and certificates to celebrate student progress. After continuing the program for a second year with more gains in independent reading across grade levels, we concluded that the school-home partnership was essential to our success. We concluded that there were several necessary elements to a successful reading initiative. These included:

- Making reading at home a school-wide initiative with support of staff and parents.
- Setting individual, classroom, and school goals.
- Developing a student-parent school connection.
- Involving the parents in the process (parental modeling and reinforcement)
- Recording and analyzing the number of books read weekly

- Measuring progress in meeting the goal and publicly displaying the results
- Celebrating progress and success

High levels of community and parent involvement, businesses, social service agencies, and community colleges/universities all play a vital role in educating students. It was with all of this in mind that we developed a comprehensive approach to home-school-community collaboration. We knew we needed to approach our literacy initiative from all fronts, including the home front. We established a number of opportunities for parents to become involved with the work we were doing to promote literacy throughout the school. Some of these initiatives are described below:

- **Exploring Literacy and MAP Through Parents as Partners**: We met with parents to communicate about school-wide information and to provide them with strategies they could use at home to help students prepare for the MAP test.

- **Parent Reading Contract**: Parents had to sign a contract agreeing to do various activities to boost reading performance with their children Monday-Friday. They also had to ensure that the children read for a minimum of 30 minutes each evening.

- **Family Literacy Night**: We hosted a one night event during which families enjoyed supper and read together as a family. Teachers were on hand to talk about the importance of literacy.

- **Title I Monthly Parent Meeting**: All parents were encouraged to attend the monthly meeting that included a light meal, discussion of ways they could be involved in the school, information about ways to help their children with reading at home, opportunities to meet with teachers, etc.

- **Spotlight on Literacy**: Every child had an opportunity to publish a book. Parents learned about the five steps of the writing process and how they could support their child with this initiative.

- **Personal Library Bookshelves**: A parent donated a number of bookshelves that students were able to decorate and take home to house their own personal library.

- **College and Career Readiness Fashion Show**: Students spent time learning about various local colleges and discussed potential career choices. Then, we held a school-wide fashion show so each child could model their attire for their selected college or career.

- **Community Partnerships:** This was a faith-based initiative work with a local Jewish congregation that supported the school with tutors who came to tutor our students in reading and math. They also provided weekly attendance incentives, adopted 10 families for a Christmas Wish, and sponsored our Teacher Appreciation Week.

- **Partnership with Junior Achievement Program**: Junior Achievement provided training to students that focused on basic concepts of economic and showed how education is relevant to the workplace relating to entrepreneurship, financial literacy and work readiness.

- **Local Children's Hospital and Healthy Kids Express**: Health professionals visited the school to conduct some basic health screenings for the students.

These are just a few examples of the various home and community activities that we were able to implement because key stakeholders in and around the school held firmly to the belief that a good education is key to breaking the cycle of poverty for our children. These stakeholder groups held us accountable for establishing high standards and high expectations for all of our students. We worked to ensure that curriculum and assessment were rigorous and aligned with those standards. We also worked to improve our instructional practices while focusing on changing the culture of our school. All of these pieces helped us to create an environment of success and achievement that benefitted so many of our students.

Children learn best when the significant adults in their lives, i.e. parents, teachers and other family and community members, work together to encourage and support them. The need for a strong partnership between schools and families to educate children may seem like common sense, but students thrive when their parents become part of the classroom. Building a positive relationship with parents is the key ingredient if you want poverty students to improve academic performance. As society has become more complex and demanding, these relationships have all too often fallen by the wayside. Neither educators nor parents have enough time to get to know one another and establish working relationships on behalf of children. In many communities, parents are discouraged from spending time in classrooms and educators are expected to consult with family members only when a child is in trouble. The result, in too many cases, is misunderstanding, mistrust, and a lack of respect, so that when a child falls behind, teachers blame the parents and parents blame the teachers.

Principals and educators are trying every day to figure out how to build lifelong readers and how to get all kids reading at or above grade level. It is vital that we have parental support in this effort because high achievement begins at home. We know that parents and caregivers are the most influential people in the education of their children! Parents must become partners in their children's academic success. Literacy is the bedrock of academic success. Simply put, kids who read on or above grade level will perform better in school than those who read below grade. The more students know about reading, writing, listening, and speaking before they come to school, the better prepared they are to become successful readers and writers.

Research confirms that a child's motivation is the key factor in successful reading. Struggling readers tend to have a lack of motivation and do not like to partake in book-related activities. These students may have trouble selecting appropriate texts, and therefore do not like to read for pleasure. This lack of reading practice at home puts them at a definite disadvantage in school and in life.

Parents must introduce kids to books at home. It is imperative that they spend some significant time each day reading books, outside of school. Kids should have a book in their backpack, a book at the dinner table, a book in the bedroom, a book in the car, and a book in the family room. **Reading on Grade Level + Strong Family Support = Success!**

These were just a few of the steps we took to keep parents informed and involved in our literacy initiative at my school. I am confident that these efforts were key to our eventual success. Our work with the literacy initiative taught me that the complex issues facing students of poverty can be effectively addressed, but only when all stakeholders come together around a singular purpose. Without focusing on parental involvement, we would never have been able to achieve the level of success that we did accomplish.

*"You know you've read a good book when you turn to the last page and feel a little as if you lost a friend."*
                                                        *--Paul Sweeney*

# CHAPTER 7

## *Epilogue and Reflections*

I retired as principal of my elementary school a few years ago, but I found that my mission for helping all children learn to read was not ready to retire with me. I find myself in a new setting, teaching English Language Learners (ELL) in a nearby suburban district serving an ethnically diverse student body. Most of the students in my new district live in poverty.

On a recent Monday in October, I had the opportunity to work with a small group of second grade ELL students to work on Lexia Reading Core5. Lexia Reading Core5 is a personalized reading curriculum for Pre-K through fifth grade students of all abilities. Students learn, practice, and consolidate fundamental literacy skills by interacting with the online, adaptive program, receiving teacher-led Lexia Lessons. Lexia Reading Core5 covers the six areas of reading instruction, including activities focused on academic vocabulary through structural analysis. This begins with oral language and listening comprehension, building to reading comprehension (Phonological Awareness, Phonics, Structural Analysis, Automaticity/Fluency, Vocabulary, and

Comprehension).The program aligns to rigorous reading standards, including the Common Core State Standards.

As I was escorting the students back to their class, I reminded them to read 30 minutes at home every day. A female student stated, "My mom said I could not read at home, I had to read at school." I must confess I was speechless. The next day, I saw the mother bringing the student to school and I begin sharing about the school-wide reading assessment that was coming up. I mentioned to the mother what her child had said about not being able to read at home. The mother looked at me and smiled. Then she looked at the student, but did not deny that she had made the statement. I shared with the mother that her child was not reading on grade level and that she was really struggling in reading. I tried to emphasize that the student needed to practice her reading skills at home every day to be able to read on grade level. The mother said, "OK." Unfortunately, the student's reading assessment was the lowest score among her peers. Obviously, I still have work to do here!

As I think back on my experiences with the literacy initiative in my school, I can say that I'm proud of what we accomplished on behalf of our students. I can also say that I learned some important lessons about myself, my leadership, and what it takes to change the trajectory of a failing school.

Today's students are preparing to enter a world in which colleges and businesses are demanding more than ever before. To ensure all students are ready for success after high school, we were committed to using the Common Core State Standards as our guide to ensure what Robert Marzano calls a "guaranteed and viable curriculum." The Common Core State Standards establish clear, consistent guidelines for what every student should know and be able to do in English and math from kindergarten through 12$^{th}$ grade, so it just made sense that we start there.

We also knew that children who read and are read to are more likely to become life-long readers. Literacy is such a vital part of a child's education, and it takes everyone to reinforce and encourage children to read on grade level. We also believed that the best way to teach reading is by using a balanced literacy framework that involves two components. We must teach children how to read, and at the same time give them a purpose for reading.

The number one issue our students faced was poverty. The reality of poverty for the vast majority of our students was that they were coming to school every day not having the basic tools for learning. Some of our students were not motivated to achieve in school because they were so preoccupied with the stresses of doing without and living in uncertainty, so they were not reading on grade level. We knew we had to stand as a buffer between the reality of poverty our children experienced every day and their need for an education that is founded in high standards and high expectations. Educators are not adequately trained to work with children living in poverty, so they often feel embarrassed, hopeless, and powerless, defeated because they can't manage the students' behaviors. The students talked back, argued with their teachers, and enjoyed having the last words. I knew I had to provide support for our teachers to help them develop effective strategies to manage their classrooms so that an environment of learning could flourish.

Educators are often not prepared to teach reading effectively, and this was certainly the case in our school. We knew we also had to focus on intensive professional development for our teachers in the effective delivery of balanced literacy and assessment to diagnose specific reading struggles children were experiencing. There was no argument among our staff that reading is essential to success in the complex world of today and tomorrow. We all knew that the ability to read is highly valued and it is important for personal, social, and economic well-being. We just had to find ways to support our teachers as they worked to develop the knowledge and skill to provide the kind of tailored, quality instruction so crucial to helping children become successful readers.

We tackled this challenge of transforming our teachers into master reading teachers by first acknowledging that teaching of reading is knowledge-based. Although teaching is an art, it is also science. Within the last several decades, great strides have been made in understanding how students learn to read. For instance, we know that students need ample opportunities to practice the skills and strategies they are learning with a variety of texts and genres. We know that comprehension instruction should include attention to vocabulary development, background knowledge, text structures and thinking strategies. We designed our professional development around teaching teachers these strategies. We also used our professional collaboration time to discuss specific challenges we faced in trying to help our children become successful readers. It was hard work and it required everyone to commit to the effort.

While we tackled our challenges by focusing on professional development and support for our teachers, we also knew that we could not accomplish what we needed to do without additional support. So often, in high poverty schools like ours, parents, guardians, or caregivers may be stressed out due to their own mental health issues, working multiple jobs and they are not able to take off their jobs to be involved in their child's education. The relationship between poverty and education is complex, but we know that education helps people make healthier and smarter decisions about their children, their livelihoods and the way they live. So, we actively pursued parental support through parent education, opportunities for special recognition, incentives, and ongoing communication. We wanted our parents to begin to see that education is not only a way to escape poverty. It is a way of fighting it.

As a reflective practitioner, I found myself always questioning the direction we were taking, and seeking what the research had to say both about effective reading instruction and how best to work with children living with all the challenges being poor brings to their lives. Over the course of our work, I constantly had to return to the moral purpose that drives me. I wrote myself a pledge to hold myself accountable to this work. My pledge to my students and my school community was:

- Place the student first in all decisions.
- Hold the same expectations for each child as if they were your own.

I also knew that I needed to focus on continuous professional development for myself so that I would have the tools and resources I needed to support my students, teachers, and other stakeholders. I focused my professional development on the ten qualities of an effective School Turnaround Leader Competencies for Success:

- Communication Skills
- Teamwork Skills (works well with others)
- Initiative
- Interpersonal Skills (relates well with others)
- Problem-Solving Skills
- Analytical Skills
- Flexibility/Adaptability
- Leadership Skills
- Self-confidence
- Strategic Planning Skills

I learned a great deal about myself through this process of personal professional development. I learned that my leadership style is shared leadership. I am committed to sharing decision making with teachers and providing opportunities for them to serve as leaders. Leadership is shared and distributed among formal and informal leaders. I am elated that my Reading Recovery training and the New Leaders Aspiring Principal Program trained me how to promote the success of all students. The following two questions have guided my leadership practices: Are the students learning? If students are not learning, what are we going to do about it? The focus on results; the focus on student achievement; the focus on students learning at high levels, can only happen if teaching and learning become the central focus of the school and the central focus of the principal.

As I explained before, our school's performance qualified us for a School Improvement Grant (SIG), and The School Turnaround Model was the framework used for our work with the resources provided by the SIG. The School Turnaround Model is a dramatic and comprehensive intervention for low-performing schools that has been shown to produce significant gains in achievement. The mission is to take charge of a failing school or struggling school and try to turn it into a model institution.

After spending three years in the SIG program, I found the "Turnaround Principal" to be an effective model for school level leadership to improve your capacity, select the best teachers and improve student performance in literacy. The emphasis is rapid, dramatic changes that result in significant improvement. As a School Turnaround Principal, I learned strategies to identify the academic areas, school conditions, and instructional practices that need improvement. I reviewed data about teachers' strengths, and weaknesses that affect instruction and school culture. I analyzed data personally, so I really knew what needed to change for our students and our teachers to achieve greater success. Through my work with the School Turnaround Model, I learned that it is possible to change the trajectory of a school, but it takes bold leadership, persistent focus on achievement, and ongoing, high quality collaboration among team members.

The literacy initiative at our school was an effective tool to implement school-wide change in a high-poverty neighborhood that faced persistent challenges to motivate students. The initiative also demonstrated to teachers, parents, community members, and external partners that by collaborating together, we could improve student performance and meet AYP on the MAP.

The Reading on Grade Level initiative helped us analyze our data and improve our reading practices. My strategy to turning around the school was to first look at the data to identify learning achievement gaps. We then looked at the research about the most effective instructional strategies to close the achievement gap. Then, we built a collaborative culture and empowered team members with data analysis, standards, and effective pedagogy. We posted our data because we knew that visible, early wins were critical to our success. I also knew as a leader that early wins were critical for motivating my staff and disempowering naysayers.

I also learned the importance of "Appreciate and Celebrate!" We celebrated daily, weekly, and monthly by formally recognizing individual students, staff, team members, and parents for their effort and hard work. I learned that it is very important to show your appreciation for the people that support you. Celebrating an individual's efforts and accomplishments also makes the other person feel a sense of pride. The whole school celebrated when evidence emerged that students were on track for reading on grade level or making improvement. We celebrated our success and we set SMART goals to improve student performance monthly on the STAR reading test, benchmark, and teacher made assessment.

As I have stated before, our greatest challenge was to help students increase students reading proficiency, getting them to read on grade level, despite the dire circumstances most of our students faced in their daily lives due to poverty. We tackled this by working to increase parental involvement support for reading at home. We worked to keep critical communication open by hosting parent meetings and providing reading strategies to help parents support their child with their monthly reading goal.

Teachers had to submit their weekly reading logs to me so I could monitor progress to determine which students or classroom teachers were not encouraging students to read at home for 30 minutes daily. I also had to communicate with parents about the weekly reading logs, Parents' Contract, and the Reading on Grade Level chart. This strategy provided me with conversation with my team members, superintendent, assistant superintendent, parents, community members, and community partners about the trajectory of each student reading levels or classroom teacher.

We also worked to increase community partnerships by constantly seeking business and community partners, volunteers, tutors, mentors to assist with academic achievement, particularly in the areas of reading and math, to help us improve student performance.

We faced some additional challenges beyond dealing with the issues of poverty. We had a relatively high percentage of ELL students, so we had to address that need through focused professional development and by securing additional resources to assist with language barriers. Professional development for teachers and staff focused on non-linguistic representations strategies to support ELL students with reading on grade level.

In conclusion, it takes the right person with the motivation and willingness to develop the skill set to lead and work in a high poverty school. I learned that it is necessary to have a high level of competency to be successful and promote the success of all students. The competency for success is a pattern of thinking, feeling, acting, or speaking to be successful in a job or role. Competencies may be developed, but they are most powerful when used to select people who are already a good fit for the job. The actions of a "turnaround" principal determine whether or not positive results will be realized. I learned that I needed to have a clear understanding of how my own competencies, strengths, and weaknesses impacted my teacher-leader team, our academic instructional coach, literacy coach, and reading specialists. I learned that I needed to be very strategic in the hiring and delegation process for each of these roles, always focusing on selecting individuals based on their competencies. These team members were critical because they formed the front line in our strategic planning efforts, and I relied heavily upon them to create successful school turnaround. Our work focused on a few early wins that built momentum, broke organizational norms or rules to get new results. In the process, we quickly learned what worked and what didn't work. We also learned how to manage a rapid pace of change because our students did not have the luxury of time for us to "get our act together" so that we could provide them a quality education at some point "down the road." They needed us to be effective right then! Traditionally, we expect change of this magnitude to take place over several years, but we made it happen right away!

As I reflect on the literacy initiative I did keep my pledge about:

- Placing the student first in all decisions.
- Holding the same expectations for each child as if they were your own.

Although I have had a plethora of training on how to be an effective principal, I must confess the Turnaround Leader Model was the most challenging and rewarding leadership position. I will always be a Champion for Kids!

"Every child deserves a champion - an adult who will never give up on them, who understands the power of connection and insists they become the best they can possibility be. I am delighted to be able to serve in a neighborhood school where the students were not reading on grade level and today the school is currently fully-accredited and meeting AYP targets.

# APPENDIX A

## *20 Ways to Encourage Reading*

Here are some ways to turn a young reader's reluctance into enthusiasm:

1. Scout for things your children might like to read. Use their interests and hobbies as starting points.

2. Leave all sorts of reading materials including books, magazines, and colorful catalogs in conspicuous places around home.

3. Notice what attracts your children's attention, even if they only look at the pictures. Build on that interest; read a short selection aloud, or simply bring home more information on the same subject.

4. Let your children see you reading for pleasure in your spare time.

5. Take your children to the library regularly. Explore the children's section together. Ask a librarian to suggest books and magazines your children might enjoy.

6. Present reading as an activity with a purpose - a way to gather useful information for, say, making paper

airplanes, identifying a doll or stamp in your child's collection, or planning a family trip.

7. Encourage older children to read to their younger brothers and sisters. Older children enjoy showing off their skills to an admiring audience.

8. Play games that are reading-related. Check your closets for spelling games played with letter tiles or dice, or board games that require players to read spaces, cards, and directions.

9. Perhaps, over dinner, while you're running errands, or in another informal setting, share your reactions to things you read, and encourage your children to do likewise.

10. Set aside a regular time for reading in your family, independent of schoolwork the 20 minutes before lights out, just after dinner, or whatever fits into your household schedule. As little as 10 minutes of free reading a day can help improve your child's skills and habits.

11. Read aloud to your child, especially a child who is discouraged by his or her own poor reading skills. The pleasure of listening to you read, rather than struggling alone, may restore your child's initial enthusiasm for books and reading.

12. Encourage your child to read aloud to you an exciting passage in a book, an interesting tidbit in the newspaper, or a joke in a joke book. When children read aloud, don't feel they have to get every word right. Even good readers skip or mispronounce words now and then.

13. On gift-giving occasions, give books and magazines based on your child's current interests.

14. Set aside a special place for children to keep their own books.

15. Introduce the bookmark. Remind your youngster that you don't have to finish a book in one sitting; you can stop after a few pages, or a chapter, and pick up where you left off at another time. Don't try to persuade your child to finish a book he or she doesn't like. Recommend putting the book aside and trying another.

16. Treat your children to an evening of laughter and entertainment featuring books! Many children, and parents too, regard reading as a serious activity. A joke book, a story told in riddles, or a funny passage read aloud can reveal another side of reading.

17. Extend your child's positive reading experiences. For example, if your youngster enjoyed a book about

dinosaurs, follow up with a visit to a natural history museum.

18. Offer other special incentives to encourage your child's reading. Allow your youngster to stay up an extra 15 minutes to finish a chapter; promise to take your child to see a movie after he or she has finished the book on which it was based; relieve your child of a regular chore to free up time for reading.

19. Limit your children's television viewing in an effort to make time for other activities, such as reading. Never use TV as a reward for reading, or as a punishment for not reading.

20. Not all reading takes place between the covers of a book. What about menus, road signs, food labels, and sheet music? Take advantage of countless spur-of-the-moment opportunities for reading during the course of your family's busy day.

# APPENDIX B

## *Reading Tips for Parents*

1. Talk to your child to help him/her learn to speak and understand the meaning of words. Point to objects that are near and describe them as you play and do daily activities together. Having a large vocabulary gives a child a great start when he/she enters school.

2. Read to your child every day starting at six months of age. Reading and playing with books is a wonderful way to spend special time with him/her. Hearing words over and over helps him/her become familiar with them. Reading to your child is one of the best ways to help him/her learn.

3. Use sounds, songs, gestures and words that rhyme to help your child learn about language and its many uses. A child needs to hear language from a human being. Television is just noise to a child.

4. Point out the printed words in your home and other places you take your child, such as the grocery store. Spend as much time listening to your child as you do talking to him/her.

5. Take children's books and writing materials with you whenever you leave home. This gives your child fun activities

to entertain and occupy him/her while traveling and going to the doctor's office or other appointments.

6. Create a quiet place, special place in your home for your child to read, write and draw. Keep books and other reading materials where your child can easily reach them.

7. Help your child see that reading is important. Set a good example for your child by reading books, newspapers, and magazines.

8. Limit the amount and type of television you and your child watch. Better yet, turn off the television and spend more time cuddling and reading books with your child. The time and attention you give your child has many benefits beyond helping him/her be ready for success in school.

# APPENDIX C

## *Parental Involvement is Key to Student Success*

1. Academic achievement increases when parents are involved in their children's education. The more intensively involved the parents are, the greater the positive impact on academic achievement.

2. Parental involvement leads to better classroom behavior. Parental involvement not only enhances academic performance, but it also has a positive influence on student attitude and behavior. A parent's interest and encouragement in a child's education can affect the child's attitude toward school, classroom conduct, self-esteem, absenteeism, and motivation.

3. Parents should stay involved in their children's education from preschool through high school. Parental involvement can make a positive difference at all age levels. Parental involvement tends to be the greatest with young children and tends to taper off as children get older. Studies have shown, however, that involvement of parents of middle and high school students is equally important. In high school, for example, a parent's encouragement can influence whether a child stays in school or drops out. Similarly, a child may consider going to college more seriously when parents show

interest in the child's academic achievement and talk with the child about the benefits of a college education.

4. Training helps parents of disadvantaged children get involved. Parents of minority or low-income children are less likely to be involved in their children's education than parents of non-disadvantaged children. If they receive training and encouragement, however, parents of minority or low-income children can be just as effective as other parents in contributing to their children's academic success.

5. Reading together at home greatly improves reading skills. Reading, in particular, improves greatly when parents and children read together at home. Reading aloud with a child contributes significantly to the child's reading abilities.

6. Schools can encourage parental involvement in many ways. Significant parental involvement is most likely to develop when schools actively seek out ways to get parents involved and offer training programs to teach parents how to get involved in their children's education.

7. Parental involvement lifts teacher morale. Schools and teachers benefit from parental involvement because involved parents develop greater appreciation for the challenges that teachers face in the classroom. Teacher morale is improved. Communication between home and school helps a teacher to

know a student better, which in turn allows the teacher to teach the student more effectively. Communication also helps to dispel any mistrust or misconceptions that may exist between teachers and parents.

8. Parental involvement benefits children and parents. Becoming involved in their children's education, moms and dads get the satisfaction of making a contribution to their children's education and future. They have a better understanding of the school curriculum and activities and can be more comfortable with the quality of education their child is receiving. They spend more time with their children and become able to communicate better with them. Some studies show that a parent's participation in a child's education may inspire the parent to further his or her own education.

9. Time constraints are the greatest barrier to parental involvement. Lack of time is the top reason parents give for not participating more in their children's education. Lack of time is also cited by school personnel as a reason for not seeking parental support. Thus, effective solutions to enhanced parent involvement require freeing up time of parents and teachers or finding ways to work around their schedules.

# Appendix D

## *Tips for Being an Involved Parent*

1. Read with your children and talk with them about the books and stories you read.
2. Help your children work on homework assignments.
3. Organize and monitor a child's time.
4. Tutor a child with materials and instructions provided by teachers.
5. Attend and actively support school activities.
6. Volunteer in classrooms, on fieldtrips, or for special events.
7. Continue to be involved when your child is in middle and high school.
8. Attend parent-teacher meetings.
9. Talk with your child about school on a daily basis.
10. Be an advocate for your child to make sure that the child's needs are being met.
11. If a problem arises, address it quickly by requesting a meeting with the teacher.

12. Advise the teacher of any issues at home that may affect the child's performance.

13. Vote in school board elections.

14. Encourage your children's success and support them when they perform poorly.

15. Take classes at a community college or adult education program to demonstrate to the child that learning is important.

16. Participate in PTA or other parent organizations, school advisory councils and committees.

17. If your child's school does not have a program for reaching out to parents, become an activist and persuade the school or school district about the importance of parental involvement'

18. Consider involving grandparents, who may be retired and have more time, in their grandchildren's education.

# Bibliography

"Are Schools Responsible For the Prison Pipeline?" (2007). *American School Board Journal*, 194 (4), pp.19

Bainum, B. (2013). *Third Grade Matters 20 Ways to Encourage Reading* Parent Guide Brochure, Commonwealth Chronicle 11 (5)

Caravette, L. (2011). "Portrait of the Reader as a Young Child". *Children & Librarians: The Journal of the Association for Library Service to Children*, 9 (2), pp.52-57. "Understanding the Stages of a Child's Literacy Development"

Clemmitt, M. (2008). *Reading Crisis? Do Today's Youth Read Less Than Past Generations?* In C.Q. Researcher, Issues in K-12 Education, Washington, DC: CQ Press

Day-Bullmaster-Day Marcella L. (2014). *How to Build a Culture that Accelerates Student Achievement*, Catapult Learning Literacy First

Fountas, I.C. & Pinnell G. S. (1999). Matching Books to Readers. *Using Leveled Books in Guided Reading*. K-3. Portsmouth, NH: Heinemann Press. Retrieved December 27, 2018 *Understanding the Stages of a Child's Litcracy Development*

Gately, Gary (2014). "Capitol Hill Roundtable: Interrupt the 'Poverty to Prison Pipeline'". Juvenile Justice Information Exchange http://www.capitolhill-roundtable-interrupt-the-poverty-to-prison-pipeline

Jensen, E. (2009). "Teaching with Poverty in Mind: What Being Poor Does to Kid's Brains and What Schools Can Do About It?" ASCD

Morrison, F. J., Bachman; H. J. & Connor, C.M. (2005). *Improving Literacy in America* (pp.173-184). New Haven, CT: Yale University Press

Winn, M. T. & Behizadeh, N. (2011). *The Right to be Literate: Literacy, Education, and the School-to-Prison Pipeline.* Review of Research in Education. 35 (1), pp.147-Winn, M. T. & Behizadeh, N

*Balanced Literacy Framework.* Retrieved from https:// www.readinga-z.com (2018)

https://www.childrenworkshops.com/sites/default/files/hgrocotto411-2.pdf

https://www.flinthill.org/wpcontent/uploads/2014/12/ResearchtoSupportMethodologies.pdf Relevant Research for Writing and Reading Workshop, Word Study – Daily Five Components

http://www2.ed.gov/parents/read/resources/readingtips.pd

http://www.2.gnb.ca/content/gnblen/departments/esic/.../what_is_poverty.html

http://www.5_facts_everyone_needs_to_know_about_the_school-to-prison_pipeline.html

*Put Reading First Kindergarten Through Grade 3* (2006). What Does Grade Level Means?

*Tips for Being an Involved Adult-Parental Involvement is Key to Student Success* http://www.publicschoolreivew.com/parental-involvement-is-key-to-studentsuccess

Read Charlotte *Grow-Your-Reader.* Retrieved from https://www.Readcharlotte.org

Research *Building Blocks for Teaching Children to Read* retrieved from http://www.readingrockets.org

https://www.yadezra.net/5-reasons *5 Reason Why Poverty Affects Behavior and Performance at School*

## About The Author

Dr. Karessa Morrow is a thirty year veteran in education. She has experience as a principal, assistant principal, literacy coach, and a reading specialist. She holds a Doctorate Degree in Educational Leadership from Maryville University, in St. Louis, Missouri.

Dr. Morrow received the Pettus Award of Excellence which recognized principals for inspiring students and staff to perform at high levels. She was a recipient of the Peabody Energy Leader in Education award which honors dedicated educators, who inspire and motivate youth to succeed in academic achievement. She is a member of Delta Sigma Theta Sorority, Incorporated.

*"There is no such thing as a kid who hates reading. There are kids who love reading, and kids who are reading the wrong books."  -- James Patterson*